Damian Smyth was born in Downpatrick, Co. Down, in 1962. He holds a doctorate in contemporary philosophy from the Queen's University of Belfast. He has edited *All Souls' Night & Other Plays* by Joseph Tomelty (Lagan Press, 1993), *Martin Lynch: Three Plays* (Lagan Press, 1996) and *John Hewitt: Two Plays* (Lagan Press, 2000). He is currently employed by the Arts Council of Northern Ireland.

DOWNPATRICK RACES

DOWNPATRICK RACES

DAMIAN SMYTH

LAGAN PRESS
BELFAST
2000

Published by
Lagan Press
7 Lower Crescent
Belfast BT7 1NR

© Damian Smyth

The moral right of the author has been asserted.

ISBN: 1 873687 87 7

Author: Smyth, Damian
Title: Downpatrick Races
2000

Cover Design: Cushnahan Design Services
Set in Palatino
Printed by Noel Murphy Printing, Belfast

for my mother and father

Remember the days of old, think upon every generation: ask thy father, and he will declare to thee; thy elders and they will tell thee
—Deut. xxxii. 7

*Now and for ever through the change-rocked years,
I know my corner in the universe;
my corner, this small region limited
in space by sea, in time by my own dead
who are its compost, by each roving sense
henceforward mobilised in its defence.*
—John Hewitt, 'The Townland of Peace'

CONTENTS

Tracks	13
The Mighty Arkle	14
Races	15
The Road to No Town	16
Downpatrick	17
Bearings	19
Bamboozelum	20
Wee Joe	23
The Loop	24
Saul	25
Veronica	26
Peninsula	27
Hey Paddy	29
Dive	30
Badgers	31
Transatlantic	32
Silks	33
Except Me	35
The Chieftain's Daughter	36
Geordie	37
Tommy	38
Big Jim	39
Shopkeeper	40
Ghosts	41
Butchers	42
Skeffingtons	43
Big Bill's View of Things	44
A Gift from Downpatrick	45
One Man	47
The Wind Among the Reeds	48
01396	49
Paddy Celtic	50
The Celtic Invasions	51
Inside	53
Haute Couture	54
Disappeared	55
Cemetery Sunday	56
Far Out	62

TRACKS

The evening he was blown up by his own bomb at the
    racecourse
he had shaved and showered as though meeting a girlfriend,
Taurus, Brut or *Hai Karate* sprinkled like myrrh on his talcy body.

Thrown off the scent, neither family nor friends could track him
    at weekends.
But the bomb that woke the birds and set the hurdles blazing
left his bed in the morning unslept in. There was nothing
    in the coffin.

Now each Easter, his name is broadcast by loudspeaker over
    the graveyard,
the wind editing the sentences of the tinny oration
that gives out buckets under the silks of flags and emblems.

On the side of the hill, among the tilting headstones, columns
    of marchers
lean as one into the camber of the uneven ground,
the brassy odour of incense drifting like smoke over the shaven
    heads.

When the breeze brings the tannoy calling the runners and riders
    miles away,
at Binns's big house in the country, where the racecourse
runs for furlongs beside the tarmac road, all you hear is bees.

There is the synchronised swimming of starlings and many trees.

THE MIGHTY ARKLE
bay gelding by Archive out of Bright Cherry

That horse bought fridges, TVs, motor cars.
It was no wonder thousands gripped the rails
when the hero hunted Mill House down again,
pulling back the earth with each great stride,

the pride of England frothing, broken, bate.
If I had a cap, I'd throw it in the air.
This was how the Irish won the war,
everything riding on every whipping boy

to face the white man down against the odds.
I have my grandda's photo of the god,
an icon, like good Pope John and JFK,
Pat Taaffe up, who, he used to say,

needed that horse 'for he couldn't sit on a stool'.
But the beefcake underneath is Cassius Clay,
the footwork perfect, the arrogance a joy,
the sucker punch a lucky horseshoe in each glove.

RACES

Stopped at Clough in their own country by an army patrol,
the brickies and joiners returning home in their cloudy clothes,
twelve miles from their native wives and clean children
        in pyjamas,

were quizzed by English voices through the machinery of visors
as baldly as Gauguin his Tahitian nymphets with lapis lazuli skin:
Where have you been? Where are you going? Where do you come from?,

as if the townland of Bright could make sense to anyone,
its two signposts staring at each other across three miles
        of rape seed,
that yellow light levelling the bad fields left fallow,

so that even an armoured car would go tacking between roadsigns
as purposelessly as the Flying Dutchman, searching for addresses.
'Downpatrick' was easier. But still the black officer

needed to push his strange face in the strange big powdery face
        of John Trainor:
'You're a big lad to be a long way from home.' The driver's white
        face an Irish mile long:
'You're not exactly sitting under the banana tree yourself.'

THE ROAD TO NO TOWN

Don't ask me what any of it means
who walked for miles to find the place it named,

turning back, obeying all the rules
of search and recovery, reading all the signs.

Where land is abandoned by the business of farms
and not a sinner left to tell the tale

then those white sheets hanging out to dry
on the hedges are blackthorn blossom.

The clocks of the tarmac tick in the summer sun
                              and all the signposts say

the three Irish miles to go are an each way bet,
though everything's in place just as it should be,

as if—as if somewhere here you'd light on what is real,
the shock of something ordinary and safe

to fix the townland fast to its own grave.
A roadway is threaded through the needle's eye of earth

and follows all the contours your maps show,
its grey old back plunging among the hills

with the certainty of purpose tarmac brings.
But the road to Bright is still the road to no town:

a bearing taken, nothing less than that,
a way not *to* or *from*, but *in* and *through*.

DOWNPATRICK
i.m. Roy McFadden

I

From here you must go uphill to the coast,
narrow hotchpotch 18th-century houses
shoulder to shoulder, holding their breath,
shuffling along the long gradients
to Killough, Ardglass, Kilclief and the seals,
to the suffering tides chewing their way inland,
black molars scattered along the sand.

The blasted trees point inwards and downhill
to a town but poorly garrisoned against the sea
that backs up over flood-gates, tide-mills, weirs,
ungagging the broad tongue of the River Quoile,
breaking through Meadowlands to the Flying Horse Estate,
streets cut adrift on the crust of marshy ground.

II

This was my home town
and we owned none of it.
English Street, Scotch Street,
Workhouse, Gaol, Asylum,
the Georgian houses of Irish Street
rising to the abattoir and the houses
where you would have found us,
drifted in from the townlands,
warming ourselves by the warm blood,
showing up messily
in *Births, Marriages & Deaths*,
living in shambles.

III

Dr. Smyth of Downpatrick, his

'rare combination of great professional skill
united to high and general attainments'
with *'botany his peculiar study'*,
is nothing to me.
                Who he is or was in 1835
is nothing compared to 'Who *would he* be?',
the cry that calls up all his ancestry,
his townland, kin and who takes heed of him,
impressing the English of the Royal Engineers,
correcting their reconnaissance,
muttering around the Barony of Lecale,
Quoniamstown, Struell, Raholp, Ballynoe,
with Lt. Rimington of the Ordnance Survey,
telling him everything.
                The local constabulary
in the dark of the morning in big damp uniforms
in our small living-room down in the Gullion,
come to bully my big rebel brother
and all the lights on like a death in the family.
Everything going into the notebooks for evidence,
at twelve years old I had nothing to say,
stammering and failing to make things not happen.
          Dr. Smyth of Downpatrick, whose
'information can strictly be relied upon
for it is from his own personal knowledge and inquiry'.

IV

'Them's wild geese,'
said old Dan Scullion, passing the Asylum,
sprawled in the back of a cart from Kilclief,
entering Down by the Gallows Hill,
bringing the town for the first time, absently,
through Michael McLaverty's *In This Thy Day*,
into the universe of things told shyly.
'In every flock you'll always get
one lad to know the road.
The rest will follow him.'

BEARINGS

The heavy water lough that laughs its way inland
is pushing its cloudy milt of ocean salt
along the river's freshwater veins,

inflating the dry marshes by the side of the new flat roads
to lap across the sandbags in the shops on Market Street,
rinsing tiles in the Bank, flooding the phone-boxes,

licking the tarmac into shape as an old landscape of ice.
At the magic wells of Struell, the natural world's at work
so that, on St. John's Eve, something must happen there

as anywhere where tidal pressure gauges are.
The pilgrims who make their way to watch the waters rise
in the pitched stone tents of eye well, ear well, bathhouse,

have come from the bookies, supermarket aisles, the Arkle Bar.
They are looking for miracles and are not disappointed:
the ghost of the ocean passes through solid ground.

When the sea goes back the seven wet miles to the coast,
along the rim of the pavements and on your shoes
a tide line of dirty salt shows the way it went.

BAMBOOZELUM

You should come to an Upper Room
in Irish Street, where four roads meet.
The room is packed and hot as a cauldron:
the men at the back and women and children
of every age, faces lit by the stage.
At the old Town Hall, fresh from Bengal
or Spain or Thailand or, further still, from dark Rathfriland
by way of Jerusalem, the Wizard Bamboozelum
brought to Downpatrick his magical hat trick,

whereby (in a fog of dry ice and confetti)
ribbons flew out of his cap like spaghetti,
furlongs of ribbons, explosions of smoke,
streamers caught on the strip lights like egg-yolk
and from under his cloak or his sleeves or his beard
sparklers caught sparks and the people cheered,
colours coming down like a downpour of rain
on the heads of a people who laughed like the sun.
And my granny's teeth, never secure
at the best of times, fell out on the flure
and scuttled away like crabs under chairs
where I found them after, all sticky with hairs.

That was the start. The compère was Rinty
in black tie and tails like Jimmy Durante,
the undefeated flyweight champion of the world
dancing at the microphone as the programme unfurled.
Bamboozelum nipped to the wings for a drink
(the small talk of his rings on the bottle, *clink*, *clink*)
and the tut-tut of the clergy, their tongues hanging out
wishing for magic to turn cream soda to stout.

There were other turns:
a wee girl balanced a stool on her jaw,
a man from Dundrum played hymns on the saw

(the strangest sound I have ever yet heard),
a wee boy read poems to a silent crowd.

When the great Bamboozelum came back on
—swaying a little, but not too far gone—
he didn't have to call for quiet in the hall:
the simple great art of his silence was all
that he ever needed to make magic happen:
his hands and his eyes made the afternoon deepen
and even the big lads who were fond of barracking
were stunned when he set the static crackling.
The excitement was frightening:
the lights went down and the wizard made lightning
shoot through the dusk from inside his gown
till you'd think, if he wanted, he could burn the whole town.

Bamboozelum on stage in the Town Hall for hours.
Only at the end, with the stage filled with flowers,
did he find himself stranded, drunk and alone,
reeling like a boxer hit with a stone,
stumbling all over his tulips and daffs
and falling headlong into the wings, with the laughs
of a crazy crowd alive in his ears,
his magic bedded in to our hearts for years.

That day the whole town went out in the street,
blinking in the sun, unsure of our feet,
but sure we'd been touched for ever. We knew
that from then on nothing less than magic would do.

The great Bamboozelum! The first massive deed
the town had seen since St. Patrick died.
He was exotic, and we needed that.
With his dress of red stars and his pointy hat,
we believed he had come from somewhere else
that would make us breathless and speed up the pulse:
somewhere outrageous, like Kashmir or Japan.

But years later, in the bus station, a wee English man,
small and compact and grey at the gills,
a little stooped over and old as the hills,
pulls cinnamon lozenges out of boys' ears
climbs on a bus and disappears.
And somewhere, I'm sure, in Bright or Tyrella,
an old wizard hides under a sparkly umbrella,
occasionally reaching deep into his kit
to make a wee miracle for the fun of it.

WEE JOE

Wee Joe couldn't read the football pools.
It would fall to me to call out all the names
while he would sit as marvellous as Buddha,
nodding when the gods would speak to him,
a dowser sounding out the sounds of words—
Grimsby, Torquay, Southport, Halifax:
teams of English Protestants kicking ball.

I'd solemnly draw exes next to them,
wondering at how much he knew to guess
not merely who would win, but who would *draw*.
From where he'd worked in Scotland ('A Gift from Peterhead')
the man who could not write brought back a pen:
astride the world, the great oil platforms
waded like Gulliver up to their knees in ink.

Wee Joe, farmer's son, fields in Ballynoe and Saul,
peeling his shirt off bending over drills,
displayed a scaly body scalded sore by oil,
the rich tattoos of eczema deep and pink.
Something like the patchy map of Empire on his back
—Aden, Gibraltar, Cyprus, Ulster—
the outposts of his nerves on their last legs.

THE LOOP

Where I first saw the celandine
was out at the old Loop platform,
concrete dead and afloat on the marshes,
where the rails, and now the celandine,
broke for the shore on one side,
for the town and market on the other.

Out there, in the damp house of celandine,
they buried Magnus Barelegs where he fell,
the last Norseman, pillager and King,
in the middle of nowhere, his lion shield
inside the hill somewhere, rattling
as the carriages clattered by.

The bridges over the new roads are down.
Under the wild honeysuckle is hidden
the odd sleeper, petrified, impassive as iron.
And out by the circle of stones at Ballynoe,
a station cut off when the tide of the rails went out
is holding its breath for the celandine

shuffling towards it for years along the beaten track.

SAUL
for Padraic Fiacc

I could begin to describe a circle:
the Giant's Ring; or the Grave of Ossian,
that lovely boy betrayed by the miracle
of the saint of Christ and a broken buckle.
So little it took for the Cross and Passion
to bring the natural world to its knees:
the big sky making its first confession
of rain to the soil, the grass, the trees.

VERONICA
for Martin Lynch

Because they spoiled her view of the lough
from the high stone windows of the fishing lodge,
the cabins on their hunkers down at the water's edge,

the dogs barking and the shouts of children,
wet clothes left out to dry on the whins
and weedy gardens infecting the air,

she sent the land agents in and levelled them,
turning the plots and the sculleries over, ploughing in
the cups and plates, pipe stems and clay jars,

the bits and bobs that couldn't be carried,
breaking up everything human and intact,
bequeathing it all to those engineers, the badgers.

It is hard work despising her. After two hundred years
it takes vigilance, patience and concentration
when there isn't a sign that living was done

underfoot here in the nowhere of Audleystown,
except that in summer that weed veronica
raises its ignorant blue pikes everywhere,

hundreds of them haunting the woods and the hedges,
crowding the pathways, choking the grasses,
                      getting their own back.

PENINSULA
i.m. Joseph & Lena Tomelty

All day we travelled through an empty land,
stopping here and there to test the silence

of the sun on corrugated iron and outhouse walls,
big red bricks as hot and stale as loaves.

Here and there, as the mute townlands went by,
Marlfield, Echlinville, Inishargy,

the perfect pink mosaics of scullery tiling
showed through the tough, stiff grass on the long acre:

grass so shallow, so little in control
of what had been the floor of someone's house,

that you could rip it back off stone like a scalp,
exposing everything.
                    We did just that,

bringing to the homes of those long gone
a fresh new blood of anger and sudden hurt

at something abandoned somewhere along the road:
a hearth, a seal's cry like a child, a dead man's voice.

'That's a five, shaped like a cup hook on the dresser',
John Quinn, uselessly learning to count in *All Souls' Night*

while two sons sink like bricks in the lough's black waters:
'The tree planted crooked will never grow straight.'

At Portaferry we paid our fare
and took our posts for a voyage back to earth,

leaving behind a coast of broken delph
—clay pipes, ink pots, willow blue and brown,

all washed and polished endlessly by the sea
then stacked up on the beach to dry like crabs.

The relics of ordinary lives in bits,
a thousand dressers tipped out on the rocks.

HEY PADDY

At Collins's Corner, Paddy the Cap
sat at the empty horse trough, gabbing.
A solitary army jeep swung round the road
to pull up, farting noisily in the sun.

'Hey, Paddy.' A loose-mouthed Tommy opened up.
'Paddy, where's the road to Bishopscourt?'
The five roads lay like the propeller blades
that tore the air to shreds at the aerodrome.

Imagine the Cap a small man, wise in wide boy play
of horses, dogs, shove-ha'penny, road bowls.
And this occurs in the timeless air
of conversations that should have taken place:

like young Berkeley's with the aged Malebranche
which ended with the Frenchman's seizure
as the young Turk said no to Occasional Causes
—'We Irish do not think so.'
                    'Hey Paddy, lost your tongue?'

This is Nineteen-Forty-Five or Nineteen-Sixty-Nine.
'How did ye know me name, young fella?'
                    'Hey Paddy, I just guessed.'
'Then guess yer fukkin way to Bishopscourt.'

DIVE

Hang a pin by the thinnest length of thread
until the turning earth gets hold of it
and draws it with its quiet force due north,

divining water you still have to cross:
a compass needle twitching at the ghost of the aerodrome,
the cries of airmen burning in their clothes.

On the runway of the River Quoile a crossbow bolt
has nestled in the long neck of a swan.
He turns with it for days to escape himself,

circling on the pivot of that pain. Eventually,
exhausted, his white skiff waterlogged,
he drifts beneath the canopy of the water and himself

like a parachute that just now failed to open.

BADGERS

Two badgers on the roadside
like drunk old men lain down by a stream.
One dandles its snout in the tarmac,
the other is pressing the long grass flat behind,
its fur abandoned to the wind like smoke.

Afterwards, they'd have slouched to Audleystown,
shouldering their way through hedges and barbed wire,
making dogs bark and the lights go on,
annoying every thing and every one,
padding through the dark, not giving a damn.

When we pulled up beside them for a while,
to be beside them, to watch their native, earthy faces
take the strain of being in the sun,
something of their deaths passed on to us.
The silence of the paths big creatures take,

the surprise of finding their lives next to ours
in unlikely places; their making room for us.

TRANSATLANTIC

The Yanks who touched down at Bishopscourt
came up to Collins's Corner along Stream Street,
shuffling in the gutters on each side of the road
in straggly columns of faces almost but not quite our own,
film stars, Harlem Globetrotters, saxophone players,

exactly as they staggered in Market Street
across the screen in the Grand, lounging through a war:
Bronx wit, Jewish noses, brash, different and liked;
a homeboy army occupying the quiet lives of Down
turning up in talk for years, like ghosts or eccentrics,

occasions for encounters where locals got the upper hand:
'Mind them big blacks on the road? Them's the boys.'
And, decades after, when refugees from Lenadoon
         and Hannastown
strung their dramatic wagon trains to the Flying Horse Estate,
the old Norman parishes of Ballyhornan and Inch

bracing themselves once more to be billeted on,
the 'international peace-keeping force' still meant Americans,
bloody from Cambodia and Ho Chi Minh. But it was the English,
encamped as always at Ballykinler and turned out like clergy,
their boots munching the tarmac almost, but not quite,
         like applause,

who rolled out the bales of barbed wire like brushwood.
                                       The English
familiar, predictable and unremarkable, exactly like us.

SILKS

I
Joe Louis

Forget about shuffling.
His hand speed was such
that only six inches,
left or right, was enough

to put you to sleep:
Good night, Irene.
Robeson. Owens. Sammy.
I'll see you in my dreams.

II
Best

Everything he did was arse about face.
Not running into space, he made it instead,
dropping a shoulder, unscrewing his hips,
losing his shadow, then reassembling himself

on the other side of a chicane of bodies.
Right foot or left was no odds to the onion-bag.
If he got down on his knees on the goal-line,
it wasn't to pray, but to head the ball in.

III
Bookies

In the *Irish News*, tipsters were hedging their bets,
two tribes vying for the perfect accumulator,
Red Hand and *Course Wire* at odds forever.

They are there yet, mantles handed down
from prophet to prophet, still getting it wrong,
the left hand not knowing what the right hand is doing,

like the old communities, swapping the whip-hand,
falling at the last like the Queen Mother's horse,
babbling a language only they understand:

*Brigadier Gerard, L'Escargot, The Minstrel,
Nijinsky, Red Alligator, Tied Cottage, Sir Ivor,
Churchtown Boy, King of Kings, El Gran Señor.*

EXCEPT ME

After she had eaten and to annoy wee Geordie
my blind granny would let her teeth fall out and lick them—
the biter bit—making the noises you make when you eat yourself.

To the same purpose, she would slip the *Irish News* under her,
cutting him off from Lingfield, Newmarket and Chepstow
while he'd try with a flourish to whip the broadsheet out
       like a tablecloth.

When the first TV was plugged in, thanks to her sick money,
it stayed tuned forever to Ulster Television, 'its own wee station',
forsaking the slick English in favour of coorse voices,

just as she'd sit beside the gramophone, still turning the starting
       handle,
to keep the record revolving at her own pace,
her beautiful old voice squeaking and creaking, ruining it
       for everyone ...

THE CHIEFTAIN'S DAUGHTER

Mornings when the mud rose
and leaves left footprints on a path
I'd stalk the grounds of somebody's big house,
go Crocketting through the thickest briars
catch strange disease from a boortree branch,
hack out homesteads. Or, at autumn, find
sap-made celtic bloodstains on a stone,
flee the knife-flash of sun on a closing gate,
be saved by the chieftain's daughter.

Then there would be laughter.
I'd meet my grandmother who at eighty-three
could still papoose a hundredweight of coal,
dipping like a priestess over wood
to untie a limb's tight knot with axe.
I'd watch her nodding from behind a tree
and wonder at that axe's rainbow
swinging from seventy years ago
to sink now in bark that centuries thought of.
I'd be barely ten but she'd call me out
like Weissmuller and guide my hand
to the bag of sticks, sharp-sided as a calfing cow.
I'd maybe drag it the length of me.
Then, holding her hand, my thumb
would secretly mark bones shifting
in the stretched kite of her palm.

This morning I was warned to 'mind the leaves'
in case I slipped for, being in front,
the coffin relied on me.
I walked with smooth wood against my cheek
aware of things my strength can't fix
but fit to hoist those sticks.

GEORDIE

It was because it had shrivelled his face
that the tears like lemon juice squirted out from it
on to the jammies, fresh out of cellophane,
in which my wee yellow grandda, like a spaceman,
floated skinnily, not touching the sides.

The experts gave up on the jack of all trades,
as he'd known they would. Made foreign by pain,
he was already becoming a specimen,
more an object of study than I could admit,
staring through the air between us like glass.

TOMMY

Tommy made headstones for the poor of the town,
thick fingers pinching the wee tacks in place
that fastened the wooden arch of the frames
into which he'd pour the grey porridge of plaster.
His garden was stacked: a dry dock of sails.
A virtual graveyard waiting to happen.

Each weekend he fell into the hedge,
at the very same spot, at the bend of the street,
cowping full drunk and laughing at everyone
struggling to hoist the great bulk of him upright.
The cap on his head. His big face alight.
'Where's Jack? Where's Jack? He'll see me home.'

His brother fell down for good in England,
in 1918, when the mine fell in.
From his grave in Downpatrick, where he isn't buried,
the mystery deepens on a plain headstone:
a whole town buried in lieu of a body,
Barrow-in-Furness cut deep in the paste.

BIG JIM

When Big Jim pushed his bike up from the Quoile
along the Bullseye Road's long gradient,
a man he knew was dead stepped from the ditch
to walk beside him silently for a while.

It might have been a tale from *Ireland's Own*,
an irruption of the old faith into time.
Instead, it was the truth, told cautiously:
friendship; comfort; safety; peace of mind.

SHOPKEEPER
after Seosamh Mac Grianna

I

The man who found his father on the beach
with a tide mark round his neck where the spade dug in,
a collar of brown blood as thick as dulse,
searched the whole world over for his killer,
even far inland where hill-dwellers were,
till, by and by, he met a girl with child
and the murderer whose face and hands were wet.
He traced a trail of sand back to his counter, satisfied.

Years later, he came across the child and killed it.
If you wait long enough, the chances come—
the bodies of your enemies wash ashore like seals
till it seems like genius how the symmetry unfurls.
Up in the rafters sits the jar of strange preserves
neither the son nor the father can afford.

II

The priest thought it was jam on his soutane.
But when they searched the beams, there was the corpse
as fresh as a loaf, the flesh all buttery,
from which the slow blood dripped when prayers began.
It was a miracle—so extravagant and footery
the priest of Christ saw centuries collapse
to be replaced by madness overnight.
That's why those three odd penances he set:

the bare-hand building of a bridge and church,
and the third that put the murderer on guard
for ever with his palm cupped for a bird
to nest on him, and leave an egg to hatch.
Unlikely as it sounds, it came about.
An old, sad killer still holding his hand out.

GHOSTS

Although the mourners at the funeral in Raholp
fell in behind his coffin at the gate,
the dead man from his bedroom still peeped out,
the blue wound like a feather in his scalp.

How can such things be in these strange days
when every townland, cautious of its dead,
disciplines the corpses to be sad
and not disturb the curate while he prays?

Now there are so many in the news,
the dead should travel silently to ground
by whatever means the headlines understand
and not set out to frighten or amuse.

BUTCHERS

Skeffingtons used cleavers on the meat,
slapping haunches wetly down on wood
and hacking through the bone before your eyes.

Behind the marble altar, in surgeon's gowns,
they rolled out sides of beef like concert harps
and racked up pigs like blazers off the peg.

The butcher's hand was a finger short.
The young would stare at the knuckle's tucked-in skin,
the meat hooks in the window like question marks.

SKEFFINGTONS

Or *Skivvitons*, as our own talking had it,
the ospidal, antiticks, turmits, loo-warm tea,
step-leathers, grewhouns and the vit,
a universe took shape with every estimate.

These words were like jerkins worn inside out:
still working for their keep and doing well,
with scars and stitches, nips and tucks,
swapping the big world's pattern for their own.

BIG BILL'S VIEW OF THINGS

Dismantling the railings at the top of the steps
to let down Big Bill's coffin with Big Bill in it
was how the boy's first funeral got under way,
with sons-in-law and friends of the family
making an arse of themselves with simple geometry,
forearms shaking with strain in the dark-pressed suits,
much as the undertakers had occupied themselves with angles
when bringing the silver hammer down on Big Bill's
    spindly femurs
to fold him up into the wardrobe that had to come out
    on its side:
Corner cutters, the lot of them, worse than bloody useless.

A GIFT FROM DOWNPATRICK

I

From Killough and Ardglass two roads take aim
at a cathedral raised in Patrick's name,
down the Gallows Hill and over the Dam,
picking up speed for a millennium,
in from the coast, along the Old Course,
in past the Mental and the Flying Horse,
past the holy wells at Struell and the Priory
of St. Thomas the Martyr, where the Spring of Glorie
still heals the sick at the Hospital of Downe,
then up John Street to the heart of the town,
the Gullion, on by Lynn Doyle Place
down Irish Street to the dead clock face
that turns to Saul and Kilclief up the hills
a timeless gaze, that yet never fails
to watch for three saints and their daffodils.

II

This is my town with all of us there:
the town of the Man from God Knows Where,
the Shambles Fight, the Purple and Black
on parade down Market Street and back
and shame on the man who won't stir a peg
for the great William Johnston of Ballykilbeg
or the old Archdeacon, who returned from Stormont
with whatever concession that Fenian would want.
The whole town's a shambles. For better or worse,
there's more than one rider on this old horse.

III

Fresh from the siege and Defence of Crossgar,
from the hospitals, banks and the Arkle Bar,

from Páirc Tomás Ruiseál and the Orange Hall,
from English Street, Irish, from Scotch and Saul,
inclusive and generous, eager to please,
there is a town you can live in with ease,
like Leslie Montgomery (aka *Lynn C Doyle*),
in lovely Downpatrick on the banks of the Quoile.

ONE MAN

My father *sang* at funerals.
The old people asked him to
booked him even decades ahead
when he was young and they were still fit,
and nothing would do,
in spite of family and the doubts of clergy
even as professionals shuffled the coffins
onto the shoulders of unwilling relatives,
but he would get up on his feet in the pews
to fulfil his undertaking:
to heighten the air,
telling the tale of a song so beautifully
that God would hear;
for God always hears
the word that's kept.

THE WIND AMONG THE REEDS

The wild bird my father kept in his bedroom
was a clarinet, its breathy call heard
in the afternoons over the diaphragm of oilcloth,
its one lacquered wing spreading over the town.

A bird of paradise in black and white,
the peacock tail of the sheet music flapping on the long neck,
the perfect silver vertebrae engaging
his strange pride in the Band of the Irish Guards,

a rebel heart thrilling to *The Minstrel Boy*
going up like a flock of geese from a barrack square
in Whitehall, Cheltenham or Pondicherry,
musicians drilling every note like marksmen.

But the soldiers who came to take his son away
left the old man wheezing at his door
and the coffin of the instrument upstairs
never to yield its skeleton again.

01396

In the concrete exchange in Church Street my father,
who'd lit up the kitchens all round Lecale
with churns of the paraffin that rotted his shoes,
inserted the plugs that made the connections
lighting up the switchboard like a city at night.
At Christmas, the calls came in for the townlands

from London, Vancouver, Cape Town, the old colonies
setting the ornaments astir in the dark
on bedside tables in Ballydonnity and Inch,
call-boxes exploding suddenly to life
at the foot of a lane, scaring rats in the hedges.
But the old exchanges don't work anymore.

The codes have been changed. The lines are down.
In Rostrevor, Banbridge, Newcastle, Kircubbin,
no one answers now when the phone doesn't ring.
It's the wind that sounds in the abandoned homesteads,
rattling each door and window in turn:
the old people now, in beds not their own,

dying in rest homes to the whoops and cries
of the lost souls around them awake in the dark.
But there are still ways to get through to Downpatrick,
imagining yourself in different rooms listening
to the racket of the telephone down in the hall,
then the operator's voice in the receiver,

the delph cups singing for miles on the telegraph poles.

PADDY CELTIC

My brother kicked points for Downpatrick
by just standing over the ball and drawing his boot back:
no ritual, no run up, the ball between the posts.
The umpires, my father said, would reach for their wee flags

as soon as Paddy Celtic placed the ball.
And so he passed into legend in his own town
like Oisín, doing feats of local loyalty,
throwing baskets for the *Ardglass Sharks*,

clearing soldiers from the Portofino Cafe,
being sound, outrageous and reliable,
a holy terror when angry, drunk when drunk,
knowing my father well and loving him.

My father in the heart ward. My brother, old beside the bed,
watching the laces of blood tying the old man to machines.
In the washing, thirty years ago, a boxing vest soaked in blood.
'Soaked in blood,' he said, 'and none of it me own.'

THE CELTIC INVASIONS

I

The radio brought Europe close to home,
reining us in by the screaming winches
of airwaves from Madrid and Hilversum
to a continent we could miss by inches,

sweeping the cross-hair over capitals.
The lives lived there were always hours ahead
and at such a pitch we needed aerials
to keep track of the subtle moves they made:

asleep in the afternoon; spaghetti
as white as tapeworms from bad tap water;
words—*confits, confiteor, confetti*;
those rows of skinny people led to slaughter.

It was the war again: *Take that, the Hun!*
Everything learned about Charles de Gaulle,
Sebastian Cabot, the Singing Nun,
the *Dreikaiserbund*, Astérix the Gaul,

falling perfectly into its own place,
old sites of conflict like penalty spots,
the slippery hordes of Holland and Greece
fleeing before the solid Ulster-Scots.

II

I moved men across the green felt map
of *Subbuteo*, like Caesar in his tent
frustrating the French with an off-side trap.
The right move now and those long years spent

inventing victories in small backyards
would come to pass like a new Quattrocento:

a language somehow less than words,
more lasting than bronze or Esperanto:

*Dukla Prague, Twente, Dynamo Dresden,
Go Ahead Eagles, Ajax, Bayern Munich,
Eintracht, Utrecht, Parma, St. Etienne,
Ujpest Dozsa, Basle, Grasshoppers Zurich.*

INSIDE

The night the cages caught fire in Long Kesh
and the camp went down with its lights on like the *Titanic*,
soldiers cleared the screws out of the wings in Crumlin Gaol
and beat the hell out of my brother.

John Henry had turned things upside down for Ireland,
for side-burns, bell-bottoms and thruppenny bits,
the years between Slade and the Sex Pistols spent
rinsing and spitting a mouthful of cracked teeth

and turning out cotton hankies embroidered with felt-tip,
of which a simple touch would send a stain spreading
like a sunburst indelibly down to the tiniest filigree.
Old Aggie Breen with no teeth, opening her son's clothes parcel

and finding inside his shirt tattooed with blood,
kept it in the hot press exactly as it was,
bringing it out as needs be, a relic for strangers,
the baffled hurt of years congealed in her homespun heart.

And John Henry put his skill at metalwork to good use,
fashioning a celtic ring from a 50-pence coin,
so turned inside itself that the Queen's head vanished,
Fidei Defensor impossibly on the inside rim.

HAUTE COUTURE

My mother speed-read the novels of her catalogues,
Empire, Great Universal, Freemans, Peter Craig,
each shiny page rattly and Bible-thin,
her fingers going from mouth to sheet like a machine

for turning pages, one thousand in a row,
their contents racking up on hangers in her head's wardrobe,
the sensible pastel fabrics setting the darkness in there crackling:
acrylic, viscose, polyester, elastane,

the Sunday best of the Ulster working classes
hers for £2.50 at twenty weeks, or £1.32 at thirty-eight.
The jaded frozen models at the end of their careers,
laughing in the sun so lightly like foreigners at home.

But visiting her guilty son in prison,
round the inside of her skirt my mother pinned,
to smuggle it in, the flag of the Republic.
Orange silk, white silk, green silk against her skin.

DISAPPEARED

Along the border, where x marks the spot,
the bodies have moulted from the black bin bags
that did them as shrouds in the hurry of night.

Now at Rossglass the seals break the surface,
the souls of the dead peering sadly ashore,
balaclavas of pelt pulled tight on their skulls.

CEMETERY SUNDAY

I

On Cemetery Sunday,
I took the top grave:
in the children's quarter,
no markers, no marble,

a half acre limbo of lumpy ground.
Backed up to the wall
by the old road to Killough,
at the only headstone,

John Linton lay down,
the tenant of the highest point
on a hillside of dead,
all County Down stretched out round him.

To my father at the middle grave
and my brothers at the bottom
was the small matter of a hundred years.
His grandmother, uncles and his father

had each laid down whole lives beneath our feet.
Still between the brackets of one century
a dozen fragile lives proliferate.

II

Unlike the Maxwells, Bretts, Southwells and the Fordes,
the poor have little history in a place.
To have their corpses handy to the door,
they'd move the sick in the Workhouse to the ground floor
so the cart that brought the oats in from the town
could carry their bodies out to unmarked graves
in two acres of lumpy ground on the Strangford Road.

There certainly is a tale of the cathedral singing,
Dickensian cabinet-makers, of aprons and top hats
and daffodils in spring round the family vaults,
the solidity of monuments; but I can't clear my head
of the fog of holocaust beneath that gentleness,
the dead piled up like turf against the wall,
the Asylum's invisible graveyard at the Model Farm Estate.

III

Because for years he'd worked the roads,
carting the pitchers of paraffin for the lamps
from lane to lane, the small farms
lit like fireflies among fields at dusk,
he'd know their people, the patients,
the sons and daughters who died on their own
in the electric light and central heat
of the Mental decades after.

And so, an orphan, he would take himself
and the pitch of his voice
round to the chapel for an empty Requiem,
alone in the pews, to light up the dark
with the lamp of his singing
flickering and swinging in the catch of his breath.
He knew their people. Remembered the kindness
of tea in their kitchens. My father.

IV

By the time I came, the runt of the litter,
sickly and thin and as odd as sin, everything was gone.
Except the tales, which turn out to be everything,
the Fenian Cycle, Spoon River or the Tain
gone forever, but still so close

you could smell the pipe smoke off the furniture,
the big men in caps and the big-thighed women

standing for moments between you and the light
then passing so silently up to the graveyard
to leave you behind with the big deeds done:

> Edward Potter groping for the rat
> blindly high up on the darkest shelf
> behind the pots and jars in the Lodging House
> and bringing it out with its mouth alive;
> the Yella Fella in his bright check suit;
> Big Jim lifting hot coals from the hearth
> and placing them gently back on the blaze,
> the smell of skin; my great-grandmother
> with basins of porter like great-bladdered Emer.

To see my dead grandfather in the *Down Recorder*
('Write in if you know who these characters are')
not having known him, but having his bearing
on board my own body like a hat or a coat,
is shocking and strange, like seeing myself
for the first time old and stout and kind,

a kind of future on offer from features
that have waited for God on the Killough Road
for most of a century.
                         He comes to me,
if I am tired and on my own,
a broad back something like my own.

IV

Tommy Smyth
        had 7 children
        5 girls & 2 boys
2 of the girls were Mercy nuns in Halifax
1 is dead, 1 other girl, Rosaleen, was a teacher in Bonecastle
The 5th girl, Kess, was a medical person in the Royal
        Victoria Hospital.

Of the 2 boys, 1 died young.
The other worked in a bank in Comber.
He is deceased.

VI

My great-grandmother's Lodging House
at the top of the Shambles in John Street,
took in those travellers on their way through
the City of Down to the coast, or inland
to the richer pastures from off the boats.
On the very site, where the roads still break

to Ardglass and Killough on left and right,
the Hospital of St. John of the English
spread with the Leper House of St. Nicholas
low buildings out along the hill, their orchards
and cells staring across the flooded valley
to Patrick, Brigid and Columcille

whose bones are thrust like the roots of trees
into the sanctuary of God's earth,
one crowded grave for the three of them
under the Cathedral's plain square haunches.
In the end, where those bodies are
is neither here nor there; not to have

the good fortune of headstones
is not unusual enough to remark upon
in the City of Down or the Barony of Lecale
or the massive parish that passes for Ulster
where a signpost will point far off to the townland
whose boundaries you are within already

and the dead turn up where they're least expected,
in school playgrounds; or are lost forever
below grid references no one can remember.
The Hospital of St. John of the English,

by right and charter from the conquest of Ireland,
could seize itself of a certain custom

whereby the Prior could dip his tureen
for two large measures (of uncertain amount)
in every brewing of ale in the City.
                    Here, Mr. Trotter in 1728
'making a new garden on Chappel Hill ...
found vast quantities of human bones
which he deposited in one large grave'.

VII

John Linton's son lies in Rawalpindi
in the colours of the Inniskilling Fusiliers

and Henry Smyth's at Ladysmith
and Bernard, underground in Barrow-in-Furness,

is my father's twin in the scarf and flat cap
he's wearing for the camera in 1918,

the year the mine collapses on him,
nine years before my father's born.

I know these people. Their faces are mine
and I take my place by the vacant graves

because the bones of your people count
and because the shadows of their features pass

across your own down a hundred years
and happiness and heartbreak simply count.

They swarm like bees to the honey of blood,
mustering like demobbed infantry in the yard

and each bangs in turn on my scullery door
to be let inside, to be out of the cold:

Warren Stranney, Mary Owens, Edward Potter, Tommy John,
McGrorys, Connollys, McKeevers, Galbraiths,
Irvines, McKennas, Lavertys, Lennons, Kellys,
and all of the people who passed through the Lodging House,

and all of the clergy who served in the Parish,
and all of those who died in the Troubles

Those souls I never knew and have forgotten.

FAR OUT

From Binns's big house, it's miles to the grandstand
where the tannoy fizzles tinily like a bee.
That makes do as a warning
that out of clear skies thunder is coming.

Then it's like nothing is suddenly happening.
The birds stop singing. Grasshoppers cease
flogging their backs, as if watches have stopped.
For down at the turn, thoroughbreds are driving

their clamour ahead of them, flushing the hedgerows
of starlings and fieldmice, ahead of their time.
When the noise and the horses collide where you're standing,
with so much muscle at work under skins,

the eye takes them in like a frieze or mosaic.
It's ecstatic: the animals are carved out of forests,
adrift like galleons with sails of pure silk,
the jockeys scampering high in the rigging.

Out here, where now so much is at stake
it is still massive suffering and cold endurance
on the *Pinto*, the *Niña*, the *Santa Maria*,
that's discovered in binoculars from oceans away.